THE SCENTED
CANDLE WORKSHOP

NIKO DAFKOS & PAUL FIRMIN

THE SCENTED CANDLE WORKSHOP

Creating perfect home fragrance, from wax to wick

NIKO DAFKOS & PAUL FIRMIN

PHOTOGRAPHY AND STYLING BY ANNA BATCHELOR AND TAMINEH DHONDY

"Thousands of candles can be lit from a single candle, and the life of the candle will not be shortened. Happiness never decreases by being shared."

– from The Teachings of Buddha by Bukkyō Dendō Kyōkai

An Hachette UK Company
www.hachette.co.uk

First published in Great Britain in 2019 by
Kyle Books, an imprint of Kyle Cathie Ltd
Carmelite House
50 Victoria Embankment
London EC4Y 0DZ
www.kylebooks.co.uk

ISBN: 978 0 85783 6748

Distributed in the US by Hachette Book Group, 1290 Avenue of the Americas,
4th and 5th Floors, New York, NY 10104

Distributed in Canada by Canadian Manda Group, 664 Annette St., Toronto,
Ontario, Canada M6S 2C8

Publisher: Joanna Copestick
Editor: Tara O'Sullivan
Editorial assistant: Isabel Gonzalez-Prendergast
Design: Hart Studio
Photography: Anna Batchelor
Props styling: Tamineh Dhondy
Production: Lucy Carter

A Cataloguing in Publication record for this title is available from the British Library

Printed and bound in Italy

10 9 8 7 6 5 4 3 2

CONTENTS

Introduction 6

Fragrance and Memory 14

Materials 30

Creating a Scent 56

The Workshops 70

Candle Safety 136

Resources 138

Glossary 140

WHO
WE
ARE

We set out on our creative pathway in 2014. Having lived in London for a number of years, we had both independently, and as a couple, dreamed of doing something a little more tangible than our day jobs in advertising. It's not to say that we didn't find our jobs interesting or exciting, it's just that we spent most of our weekends trawling the local markets and amazing independent retail stores of London and beyond for one-off finds, and felt that there was a whole other, hands-on world of creativity that existed but to which we had no access.

One day, while speaking with a regular trader at Netil Market in London's East End, our favourite market, we discussed starting our own stall. We took the details of the manager of the market and applied as 'Earl of East London'. At that point, Earl of East London was a Tumblr that Paul had created in order to stay in touch with colleagues from a previous job. It was those colleagues that really came up with Earl of East – it's the name with which they had baptised Paul because he constantly tried to convince the entire office to move to East London.

Coming back to our market application, though. We were over the moon when we were accepted to run a trial stall at the market just six weeks later. We spent that time curating our offerings and repeatedly testing our table set-up. It was only then that we realised how important scent is to us. We know this might sound strange, but despite living together and constantly filling our home with candles and incense and buying perfume, we hadn't really ever spoken about scent. So that was the moment when we decided our stall would focus on candles (and more broadly, scent), cacti and curiosities; essentially, all of the things we love. We bought in a selection of the best independent brands and one-off finds and figured that if the stall didn't go well, at least we had bulk-bought all of our favourite things!

The first market day came; we were blessed with the weather, and having set up the display many times in our kitchen we probably looked way more organised than we really were. The stall was well received, but it was when our first customer, and now friend, Adam Reed came by and bought half the stand that we got the confidence boost we needed to continue.

That one-off stall soon became a regular feature in our lives, but more importantly it gave us access to the creative community we had been longing to join. However, just a few months in, we felt something was still missing. You see, curating our stand was great, and we knew we had found our niche with scented products, but being surrounded by so many amazing artisans made us crave making our own thing, and with it starting our own brand under the Earl of East London name. We knew that whatever that thing was, it would need to be scent-based, and having quite literally tested the market, we knew people responded very well to interior fragrance.

So, much like we hope you will after having read this book, we set out to learn how to make our own scented candles. We did our research and bought all of the basic kit to get started in our kitchen – which pretty quickly became a testing lab!

At the same time we decided to take on and convert a small shipping container within Netil Market. After all, this was where it had all begun and we figured it would be the perfect studio and weekend shop (it only ended up fulfilling on the shop part), which meant we had a place where we could sell our brand. The defined deadline of our opening really pushed us to launch our own line, so by May 2015 we felt we had three scents good to go, we had found the perfect vessel in which to make the candles, and we worked with a local graphic design student to create our logo and label. In July 2015, we launched.

We didn't really know what to expect from that point. There was no grand masterplan, we just wanted to do something we enjoyed and see where it went. We fell in love with creating – we developed a scent for a friend's wedding and had a request to create a custom scent for a local independent brand. The candles were doing very well at our own shop and we began getting wholesale requests. It all happened very quickly and by the end of that first year we had 25 stockists.

If we've learnt one thing on this journey, it is to go with it – every spare moment became about our brand, and our evenings were spent pouring candles in our makeshift studio in our home. Our weekends were spent delivering orders and trading at our market and at other events across town, and we loved every moment.

ABOUT OUR WORKSHOPS

We'll provide you with the skills and confidence to start developing scents that are completely unique to you.

At the beginning of 2016 we decided we wanted to share our craft with others. Making our candles at home was no longer feasible because our whole home had turned into a production line, so we took on our first studio and finally had a dedicated space where we could run candle-making workshops every weekend. We didn't really know how that would go, but we consistently filled each class and realised early on that the desire we had to do something a little more tangible was quite widespread, and that we could inspire others to start out on their own creative pathway. The classes quickly became our favourite part of the weekend, allowing us to meet like-minded people and help them to learn a new craft.

Fast forward to today and we have taught all over Europe, with our stockists, for brands and at events. It never gets old. Many of the people who have attended our classes have been there for every scent launch and when we have opened our new stores, and they have become friends. And that leads us to this book; we hope we can share our craft with all of you, and that you too can start to develop your own fragranced candles so that this becomes 'your thing'.

During the course of this book we will provide you with all the knowledge you need in order to craft your own beautifully scented candles. You will discover that making a candle is extremely therapeutic. You need to learn to slow your pace, take your time and follow all of the necessary steps so that your candle is blended correctly to ensure an even scent throw (the fragrance being emitted by the candle), a clean burn and a beautifully presented candle.

Much more than just a series of recipes, we will provide you with the skills and confidence to start developing scents that are completely unique to you, your memories and experiences. It is here where you will learn how to show your flair and create something completely personal for you, your home or your loved ones.

We have shared a few workshops to help you create candles for lots of different situations – whether that is a seasonal scent, or something for a special occasion such as a wedding – along with some of the insider tips that we have learnt along the way. By the time you've finished reading, you will have all the tools you need to create layered scents and beautifully hand-crafted candles.

FRAGRANCE
AND
MEMORY

A BRIEF HISTORY OF SCENT AND FRAGRANCED CANDLES

Let us start by saying that we are by no means historians, or scientists. We are completely self-taught, so when we started out on the journey to launch our own line it was important for us to look at the history of scent and do our research simply as a point of reference. This allowed us to add some context to what we were doing and to better understand why fragrance is so important for many of us. As we delved deeper into the world of scent, the whole thing became more and more interesting, but read on to find out for yourself.

The world of scent has always been primarily linked to religion, purification and spiritual rituals. In around 3,000 BCE, it was Egyptian priests who were believed to have been the first to use aromatic resins to scent spaces during ceremonies, believing doing so would connect them and the people around them to higher powers and spiritual beings. Ancient Egyptians were also known to be the first to use rushlights – torches made of reeds or sticks soaked in animal fat that could either be carried or stuck into the ground during religious celebrations. It was not quite a candle as we know it today, but it was pretty close, and it may even be the first version of a taper candle. Fragrance and candlelight were not only used during religious ceremonies, they also became part of everyday life in Ancient Egypt, with fragrance becoming a sign of status, beauty and health – the health aspect pretty much laying the foundation for what we now consider to be aromatherapy. [1]

Other ancient civilisations – including the Romans, Greeks and Chinese – also celebrated fragrance, for use in their religious ceremonies. These people believed that scent came directly from the gods and, like the Ancient Egyptians, they were under the impression that it would connect them to higher powers. Based on the sacred ideology around fragrance, the Greeks explored scent further and were the first to create fragrances to be worn on the skin, which were made by extracting natural oils from plants through pressing. The Greeks were also amongst the first to associate fragrances with hygiene and medicine. The Romans, on the other hand, were more focused and hence quicker to develop what we today would refer to as a taper candle, using papyrus as a wick over which they poured melted wax [2]. At that point, the most commonly used waxes were tallow, which was fat from cows and sheep; beeswax; or waxes obtained from other insects and trees.

The world of scent has always been primarily linked to religion, purification and spiritual rituals.

Similar candles made out of insects, nuts or plant waxes with rice-paper wicks originated in Asian countries. In addition to this, the Chinese made candles from whale fat, while in India you would boil the fruit of the cinnamon tree to obtain wax. [2.1] These are probably the first documented candle-making processes of a naturally scented candle.

Over the centuries, with all the transformative historical episodes and developments that occurred, the world changed. The opening of the Silk Roads allowed sudden access to spices and incense from the Far and Middle East for the Western world, as well as new types of flora and fauna from the African continent, not to mention new techniques and uses of scent that would come to change the world of fragrance forever. [3]

This new flow of knowledge and expertise had a huge effect on the Roman Empire, where fragrance soon became an intrinsic part of daily life. They even invented the word for it: *par fumum* meaning 'through smoke'. [4] But, unlike today, ancient perfume was based on gums, resins and oils and usually came in the form of solids. [5]

At this point, Islamic cultures in the Arab world, where scent had always played a central role in everyday life and religious ceremonies, contributed to the development of new techniques of distillation and advanced the work with new raw materials. Their geographical location and successful trade with China and the overall East Asian area, allowed them to cultivate non-native and more exotic plants and materials, while always improving the art of distillation. [6] [7]

Fast forward to the Middle Ages, when Crusaders brought back those raw materials, fragrances and perfume-making secrets from the Middle and Far East, and Europeans rediscovered the healing properties of fragrance and aromatherapy. Suddenly, doctors would use raw materials to protect themselves when treating patients and everyone who could afford to would carry a ball of scented materials, to ward off infection, as it was believed that diseases were transmitted through the air. It was also the time that saw the creation of the first ever alcohol-based perfume. However, it was the Hungarians who introduced the first modern perfume, which was known as Hungary Water. Created for the Queen of Hungary during the fourteenth century, it was made out of scented oil blended in an alcohol solution.[8]

The real breakthrough in perfume production came during the Renaissance, when the Italians discovered how to create *aqua mirabilis*, a clear substance made of 95 per cent alcohol and soaked with strong scent. This scented water led to liquid perfumes replacing the common solid perfumes. This invention made Italy, and Venice in particular, the centre of the world for perfume trade for centuries to follow. [8.1]

It was also during this time that candles made out of tallow, and later beeswax, became popular once more across Europe. Chandlers, as candle makers were called, would go door to door selling tallow tapers. Beeswax, on the other hand, was only used for the production of candles for the church and those who could afford it. Moulds were introduced for candle making in the fifteenth century in France, paving the way for candles in a variety of shapes and forms. [9]

During the sixteenth century, perfume came into widespread use amongst the monarchy, which coincided with the Italian Catherine de Medici's move to Grasse, France, together with her personal perfumer. There she started a cultural phenomenon, wearing perfume over her gloves and body. France's stronghold in the world of perfume was reinforced, as Louis XIV became known as the 'perfume king'. His fear of water and obsession with scent saw him commission new fragrances on a daily basis, which allowed perfume makers in France to explore scent-making and to blend further and further, manifesting Grasse's position at the top of perfume development. [10] Across the pond during the Colonial times, Americans started exploring candle making, by boiling down the berries from bayberry bushes and turning the resultant wax into candles, thus creating the first scented candles of the New World.

Fast forward to the nineteenth century, when, during the Victorian era, chemists discovered molecules that would transform and elevate the perfume industry. These synthetic compounds allowed perfumers to make fragrances more affordable by creating scents without the need to work with often hard-to-get, and even harder to work with, ingredients. Those breakthrough developments during the Victorian era helped British fragrance-makers improve their skill set and claim world dominance in perfume making.

Over the centuries, chemists and innovators would build upon the knowledge of previous generations, and they would discover and introduce new ways of making candles, too. The one area that went through the biggest change was in the wax used. Tallow, which up until then was the cheapest material but emitted a foul smell when lit, was banned in major European cities, forcing chandlers to look for alternatives. During the eighteenth century, whale wax was being used instead of tallow or beeswax. Soon after, the first ever candle-making machine was invented in the UK, enabling candles to become an affordable commodity for the masses. The braided, self-trimming cotton wick was introduced and paraffin entered the market as the cheapest alternative to wax. [11] Up until that point, candles and oil-burners had been the main source of light for the masses.

While it didn't take long for perfume makers and brands to move perfume into the world of lifestyle and exclusivity – turning perfume and scent into a luxury commodity – in the twentieth

The power of scent is indisputable, which is why we felt the need to explore it further when we first started our business.

century [12] the production of candles fell into decline. The invention of the light bulb and other alternative methods of lighting resulted in the demand for candles dropping dramatically. It is probably one of the main reasons why the development of scented candles didn't progress further at this point. Instead, while the world of perfumery flourished, candles almost vanished completely. With this immense decline, candle makers and the overall industry needed to find a niche, new way to market their products. So they began to make candles in different sizes, shapes and colours, marketing them as decorative items for the home rather than as a source of light. Thankfully, this tactic worked, and by 1950 people started buying candles again, to beautify their homes. The popularity of candles over the following decades meant manufacturers could explore and invest in new materials, such as soy wax, as well as finally introduce scents.

When looking at the history of scent it's easy to see the importance it has played in religious and spiritual traditions, which is still valid today. However, in more recent times scent has moved into the world of beauty and personal care, with fragrance becoming a luxury commodity that the majority of us enjoy. Candles, on the other hand, and scented ones in particular, have had a less-impressive journey. At first candles were needed because they were the single source of light, scent didn't play a huge role in their makeup and was really a by-product of the burning wax. Tallow candles smelt awful, while cinnamon and bayberry candles smelt sweet. However, in recent times, people have taken the concept of scent and applied it not just to their person but also to their environment, using scented candles to create a sense of luxury to a space.

The power of scent is indisputable, which is why we felt the need to explore it further when we first started our business. While some brands create a degree of exclusivity that makes their products seem unattainable to ordinary people, we wanted to take others and our community on the journey of scent with us; we took people from considering scented candles an affordable luxury to attending weekly workshops not just in our studio, but across Europe and the world, too. The fact that scent has only recently been introduced to candle making, while both elements have meant so much to civilisation throughout the years, made us think about the terminology of Future Heritage, which is how we like to think of our business proposition and brand. Taking a traditional craft and making it suitable, achievable and enjoyable in today's modern world and the future.

THE SCENTED CANDLE WORKSHOP

THE
SCIENCE

Whenever we develop a new scent, we're trying to capture a memory, place or feeling.

HOW DOES FRAGRANCE WORK?

This is an interesting one, and again, let's make one thing clear: we're not writing this with our scientist hats on, rather as curious individuals who wanted to find out more about the world of scent, how it all works and why it affects us the way it does in the first place. We're fascinated by the link between scent and memory, and why certain fragrances are so evocative. Whenever we develop a new scent, we're trying to capture a memory, place or feeling – making scent a very personal story.

To be able to understand how and why scent and memory are so closely linked, we first had to understand how smell works. Before we started reading up on this, we simply started chatting about the process of smelling to customers and friends, and we tried to observe how we use our noses in our day-to-day lives. You can start your own research now; think about it, when did you last consciously use your ability to smell, today or even this week? Was it when you used the open and half-empty milk out of the fridge or was it a few nights ago, when you could smell your dinner burning in the oven while watching TV? It might not have been any of the above, but simply taking a moment to think about in what context you last used your skill of smelling, will tell you so much.

Our noses are glorious, powerful tools, yet we don't pay too much attention to smell, especially when you compare it to other senses, such as vision, hearing or taste. We're all quick to discuss and review a movie we've just seen, or to criticise and deconstruct the ingredients of the meal we enjoyed a few nights ago. But when it comes to scent, we often run out of words.

We tend to use our sense of smell to make quick judgements – we like something or we don't – and then we simply move on. That's mostly because we just don't pay much attention or give it too much thought, but also because the perfume industry has created a world of expertise that we're not allowed to access. If we feel we don't have the right knowledge and vocabulary, we'd rather keep quiet and we don't tend to follow up and express our thoughts. When in reality, especially if you've read the earlier pages about the history of scent and the importance it has played in human history, it's second nature to us. All of this becomes even more apparent when you compare the human species to the world of animals. Animals use their sense of smell to simply navigate through the world, to decide which way to walk and what or what not to eat. [12.1]

But let's take it from the top. Smell is known to be the oldest sense and is the most rudimental of them all. In fact, as babies it is the first sense we begin to use, before seeing or listening. There are two ways for us to detect and pick up smells – the one we all know is through our nose and, more specifically, through breathing in molecules through our nostrils. The other way to detect scent is through our mouth, in combination with our taste buds when we eat and chew – in other words, when we use our sense of taste in conjunction with our sense of smell. If you recall having a blocked nose, food doesn't taste as good as it should, that is if you can smell it at all. That's because 75 to 95 per cent of what we experience as taste is actually what our nose tells us something smells like. [13]

Overall, smell is a complex neurological process that takes place within the human body. It involves many different parts, such as the brain, the olfactory bulb, the nasal passage, the cribriform plate, the olfactory epithelium, as well as our noses and everything they come with. Since this isn't a science book, we'll simplify it all so that you have the basics and know-how to use this natural process to develop your own candle scents.

When you, for instance, smell a flower, a baked good or your breakfast, your nose picks up those odour molecules as you breathe in. Those molecules then travel through your nostrils, get filtered and humidified and arrive at your odour cells. You have about six million odour cells that sit at the back of your nose that make sense of those odour molecules. Just as a comparison, dogs have about 220 million olfactory receptors, and furthermore, the part of their brains responsible for making sense of scent is, proportionally speaking, forty times greater than that of a human. But back to your nose and the millions of cells you've got. The cells are equipped with protein tops, which react to scent information and odour molecules, which then transmit the information via the olfactory bulb to the brain. Different receptors will react to different odour molecules and each and every single one of us will have a unique sense of smelling, with cells renewing every month on average. [14, 15]

We once read a very simplified version of it all, which is what we always share during our workshop: if you think about the scent molecules flying around the universe as keys, and the protein tops sat at the back of your noses as keyholes, every key can fly into any keyhole, but there are only limited numbers of keys and keyholes where the process of unlocking is absolutely smooth. That's also the logic of us smelling and making sense of different things such as lemons, limes and oranges, as opposed to just citrus in general.

So there you have it, that's a brief synopsis of how our noses work and why scent is so important, but why is it so closely linked to memory? Let us explain.

Smell is a complex neurological process that takes place within the human body.

THE LIMBIC SYSTEM

Now that we have an understanding of how the process of smelling takes place and how scent finds its way from the universe into our brain, it's time for us to understand how the journey continues.

We've established the fact that we don't consciously use our noses all that often. We've also established how powerful our sense of smell is, but where does this leave us?

If we continue the journey of the molecules that triggered a reaction via your odour cells and into the brain, we'll arrive at the limbic system and this is where it all gets very interesting. The limbic system is the part of the brain thought to play a major role in dealing with moods, behaviour and emotions. It is the part of the brain that stores all of your memories, but interestingly it is also the part of the brain in charge of decoding scent information. [16, 16.1]

Understanding that scent gets processed by the same part of the brain that governs emotions and stores all of our memories, helps us see that our noses are an even more precious tool. Suddenly, the historical relevance of scent in the realm of spirituality makes total sense too.

So now you have it, there really is a science behind why scent is such a strong memory trigger. We have all experienced occasions where we're walking down the street or waiting at a station for the next train and suddenly a person walking our way instantly reminds us of a friend or relative based on the fragrance that they're wearing, or we've stepped into a new space and, based on the dominant aroma, we immediately felt comfortable, welcomed and familiar, or we just wanted to get out of there straight away. But what does that mean to you and your candle making, and how can you use it to develop your own unique scents?

The limbic system is the part of the brain thought to play a major role in dealing with moods, behaviour and emotions.

SCENTS THAT MEAN SOMETHING

Now that you have an understanding of how scent is decoded by the brain, you can make a conscious decision about which world you want to play in. Whether that is aromatherapy – using scent to make you feel relaxed, energised or invigorated – or whether that is using scent as an emotional trigger to take you back to a favourite place or time.

Being self-taught has meant that we talk about scent in a simple and concise way. We believe that the fragrance industry has overcomplicated something that we are all able to decode, and that has left many of us feeling that we have no sense of smell whatsoever. But when you consciously think about what you are smelling in simple language – in terms of colours/memories/emotions – you're often surprised at how much you can actually distinguish.

From our perspective there is nothing wrong with wanting to create a simple vanilla or grapefruit scent, but we believe that the fun part of scented candle creation really is around developing your own unique fragrance. Layering notes together allows you to create something that has much more depth and can genuinely tell a story that is personal to you.

For our line we chose to focus on the memory part, and more specifically on developing scents inspired by travel and places we love. Focusing on memory allowed us to tell a story through scent, whether that is recalling memories of our grandparents' gardens, creating a scent that is a nod to London, our home city, or fragrances that celebrate Japanese bathing culture.

When it comes to storytelling, the brief you set yourself can be literal, for example, *these were the flowers in my grandparents' garden*; or more abstract, *these notes remind me of a particular thing, such as leather and tobacco leaf, which are reminiscent of a Georgian drawing room.*

Take Greenhouse, a scent in our line. Our approach here was quite literal. Greenhouse was inspired by Greece. More specifically, Niko's childhood memory of his grandmother, who was known in her village for her tomato plants. What we've worked with here is a blend that represents exactly that. It's a combination of vine tomato, lemon zest, parsley seed and basil. As people smell it, they often point out that it reminds them of gardening, some might pick up on the lemon zest and feel invigorated or just longing for summer, so it seems to have the desired effect, not just for us but for our customers.

For a more abstract approach, our Strand scent is a good case in point. It takes influence from Scandinavia and, more specifically, Copenhagen, a city that we love. We worked on this fragrance with the crisp Danish sunset and Baltic Sea breeze in mind. To showcase the depth of this scent, we deliberately created a candle whose first impression or 'cold throw', as it is also known – the scent of the candle when unlit – is completely different to its aroma once lit. Strand is one of the more complex blends in our line, comprised of mandarin rind, seaweed, birch wood and bay leaf. The best thing about this is when people actually say it reminds them of home, and home then turns out to be Copenhagen.

So there you have it, once you decide on the route you want to go down the next step is to start with trialling and testing the wide array of different fragrance oils available.

MATERIALS

TYPES
OF
FRAGRANCE

When it comes to materials and, more specifically, oils, you can read a lot and you'll hear even more on what is good or bad, but at the end of the day all you have to listen to is yourself and the brief that you've created. The final list of ingredients and materials you'll use will be influenced by what you've set up to achieve in your creative brief. We'll discuss the creative brief on pages 58–61 and provide a basic template to guide you through the process.

There are different types of oils available, which can be broken down into those that are natural and those that are synthetic. However, this really only describes how they have been created and what they are made out of, rather than the misconception that one is good and the other bad. We will break this down further for you, but again, we're not here to tell you what you should and shouldn't use, just what the basic differences are.

ESSENTIAL OILS

These are oils that are basically extracted from the flowers, roots, twigs, peels, seeds and barks of plants and trees or grasses, to name a few. To get to an essential oil, some serious devices are needed; they can be distilled or pressed out of these materials, or the botanics can be treated with chemicals.

The most common way to obtain essential oils is via steam distillation. Plants are held over boiling water, the rising steam travels through a tube, while being cooled, causing condensation and turning the steam back into liquid. The oil is then separated from the water, and there you have the essence or essential oil from the raw material.

Since they derive straight from nature, the quality of essential oils will ultimately depend on the quality of the treated plant, grass, root, etc. This is very much dependent on a number of conditions. From geographical conditions, such as weather, all the way down to methodical conditions, such as the devices and skillset being used to extract the essential oil.

While we might tend to assume that natural is better, when it comes to consistency, certain oils end up being different from season to season, region

to region, supplier to supplier and ultimately batch to batch, making it more challenging and sometimes impossible to recreate the identical scent profile for your candles. Perhaps that's not an issue if you are creating that scent once, but it could be a problem if you are creating a fragrance for sale or for an occasion such as a wedding, that you will want to create again and again.

There is often a misconception that using essential oils only is the best route; if you are playing in the aromatherapy world this is of course the logical step, however, it is worth considering the environmental impact of the production of certain essential oils. For example, it may take a huge amount of petals to make a jasmine oil absolute from the plant's tiny flowers.

SYNTHETIC FRAGRANCE OILS

Synthetic fragrance oils are created in a lab, they are man-made and they have nothing to do with how scent appears in nature. Since they are made out of synthetic compounds that are much more affordable, easier to obtain and because chemists can work with certain ingredients, they can make those oils carry scent for much longer than their natural counterpart. [17]

In addition to longevity, synthetic scents can be blended and blended to create a neverending list of scent profiles. Although they will last longer, throw scent better and give you much more to choose from, they are made out of a chemical derived from petroleum, and also contain chemicals like phthalates. These chemicals can of course be harmful and this should be a major consideration when you are thinking about scent creation and something that will be emitting fragrance into the environment.

_____

Synthetic scents can be blended and blended to create a neverending list of scent profiles.

_____

BOTANICAL OILS

Botanical oils are also known as nature-mimicking oils. Simply put, they sit somewhere between essential oils and synthetic fragrance oils, as they are based upon the structure of essential oils using only one single molecule, but they are man-made in the lab by artificial means. In other words, chemists will take the complex natural molecular structure of an essential oil, then extract, copy and replicate it all in one single scent to recreate the otherwise complex aroma.

Because they are chemically identical to the oils naturally occurring in nature, they do not contain harmful chemicals like phthalates. However, they do not have the healing benefits of natural essential oils. They do, though, have the same power to throw as something that is fully synthetic. [18,18.1,19]

Tip:

When it comes to which oils to use we can't say that natural essential oils are necessarily superior materials to work with. Ultimately it all comes down to your intentions and brief. We would, however, recommend looking for botanical or essential oils wherever possible.

TYPES OF WAX

Choosing a wax comes down to what you're intending to create. We'll explore the different types, but remember that within each of these there are many variations, dependent on the supplier you use.

When it comes to picking your wax, environmental parameters might help you make your decision. Furthermore, there will be waxes that you will find are easier to work with than others, as well as waxes that will perform better than others when blended with your scent creation. We are listing them in the chronological order of development and use, rather than as recommendation. As creators we have chosen to use soy wax in our existing line, which is our preference based on testing in combination with our scent profiles, but we recommend carrying out your own tests before making your final decision.

BEESWAX

The most traditional wax that is still commonly used today. It has retained its relevance, especially in the world of religion. Beeswax is made by bees – no surprise there – and it comes in a yellow, brownish colour with a natural honey-like scent. It is a very hard wax with a high melting point, which makes it quite difficult to work with, as opposed to some of the other waxes we will discuss. The other difficulty with beeswax is that it doesn't provide the best scent throw when blended with additional fragrance. On the other hand, beeswax emits negative ions when it burns, which are known to reduce pollution in the air that we breathe. You can buy beeswax in blocks, slabs or pebbles, or sheets that you can instantly roll into a candle.

PARAFFIN

RAPESEED
WAX

SOY WAX

BEESWAX

COCONUT
WAX

PARAFFIN

Paraffin wax was introduced to the market in 1850, and it has remained the most commonly used wax, even today. It's a white, odourless substance that is a by-product of petroleum. You can use paraffin for everything from candles in vessels all the way to pillar and taper candles. It has a steady burn at about 55 and 68°C (130–155°F). [20] Paraffin is used commonly with scent, particularly at the lower, mass-produced end of the market. In terms of the raw material for candle making, it is available in solid blocks and is the most affordable wax. It is easy to use and blend, and will provide a smooth finish when set. However, as a petroleum byproduct it is not the most health-conscious option, because it will emit toxins when burning.

SOY WAX

Soy wax is our wax of choice. Considering how long candles have been around, soy wax only surfaced in the early 1990s, with the majority of the crop coming from the US. There are a number of soy waxes that all have different melting points. Depending on what kind of candles you'll be making, you'll have to look for the right type of soy wax for a container, a pillar or taper. It is an off-white substance that can come in flakes, pebbles or solid blocks. It has a creamy consistency, which will become soft easily between your fingertips. Compared to traditional waxes, soy has a lower melting point, starting at 49°C (120°F), making soy wax candles longer lasting than those made out of paraffin or beeswax. It is also a good wax if you are looking for a clean, even burn throughout your candle.

RAPESEED WAX

Rapeseed wax acts in a similar way to soy wax and has similar qualities when it comes to scent throw and burn time. The benefit of rapeseed wax is that it is grown locally in Europe. It will start melting at around 43°C (110°F), which makes it sensitive to sunlight.

COCONUT WAX

Coconut wax is made from the flesh of the coconut and is often blended with some harder vegetable waxes, such as soy or rapeseed, to create a nice white, creamy container-candle blend, with a naturally slight coconut-like smell. Coconut wax melts at an even lower temperature, that's why it's important to add a harder wax to the blend. Due to the lower burning temperature, coconut acts in a similar way to soy wax, meaning candles made out of those waxes will last longer in comparison to those made from paraffin or beeswax.

WAX BLENDS

In addition to the pure wax variations, you'll find that brands often choose to blend waxes. This is done for a number of reasons, including burn time and cost efficiency. Manufacturers of wax are increasingly making these blends available for home and small-scale crafting, but why use a blend versus a pure wax? Well, you might blend a vegetable wax with your beeswax to bring down the melting point, or add paraffin wax to a vegetable wax to raise the melting point. All of this will ultimately have an effect on the softness of your candle and therefore the burn time of the product you're creating. [21]

When it comes to picking your wax, environmental parameters might help you make your decision.

TYPES
OF
WICKS

Simply put, the wick is the engine to your candle. If the wick is wrong, too strong or too weak, you'll have issues with your candle, its burn behaviour and ultimately its scent throw.

Wicks can come in a variety of forms and sizes. Every different-sized wick will create a different-sized flame, so with that in mind the size of the wick needs to be right for the diameter and shape of your vessel, as well as for your wax and oil combination. If the wick is too thick, the flame will be too strong and it will cause your vessel to overheat. If the wick is too thin, and the flame is too small, it will cause tunnelling (where only the central part of the wax melts, creating a shorter burn time) and will have a negative effect on scent throw.

The standard wicks you can choose from are either going to be braided, twisted, plaited or knitted. Usually they are made out of cotton and are categorised as flat, square or cored. As an alternative to these standard types there is also a range of wooden wicks available on the market. [22] So let us run through your options.

FLAT WICKS

These are used in free-standing candles such as pillars and tapers. They are designed to bend, allowing for an even burn, while self-trimming throughout the burn.

SQUARE WICKS

*The wick is
the engine to
your candle.*

Used mostly in candles made out of beeswax, or harder waxes, these also have a tendency to bend on the burn but are more rounded and robust. Square wicks are less likely to clog, too.

THE SCENTED CANDLE WORKSHOP

CORED WICKS

As the name suggests, these have cores made out of cotton, paper, zinc or tin. They are most commonly used for container candles, in which you'll need the wick to self-trim. To make sure cored wicks are rigid, they are often dipped into harder vegetable wax, making it easier for you to work with.

WOODEN WICKS

These make an innovative alternative to the standard wicks. Their burning behaviour is excellent and they throw scent as well as traditional cotton wicks. On top of that, wooden wicks will make a crackling sound as they burn, adding to the ambience.

CHOOSING THE RIGHT WICK

So how do you ensure you choose the right wick for your candle, without wasting many wax pours and a lot of fragrance and essential oil? It's actually a fairly straightforward process called the wick behaviour test.

Before we jump into the testing, there are a couple of quick but very important things to consider when it comes to wicks. We've probably all experienced a smoking candle every now and then. In most cases, it's down to us not using or looking after the candles properly, but if you're making your own, it might simply be that the wicks are not the right size. When a candle is smoking, it usually means that the wick is too large. A simple way to eliminate the smoke is to blow out the candle, allow it to reset, then trim the wick before relighting. The part that you want to trim is the bit that has 'mushroomed'. If you remove the excess wick, it will not only stop smoking and flickering, but it will also help you make your candle last as long as it should.

Wick behaviour testing, or basic burn testing, is a very quick way of finding suitable wicks for your wax and oil ratio, and ultimately candles, based on the diameter of your chosen vessel. Manufacturers will inform you about the radius a wick would burn away. But we recommend running wick tests yourself.

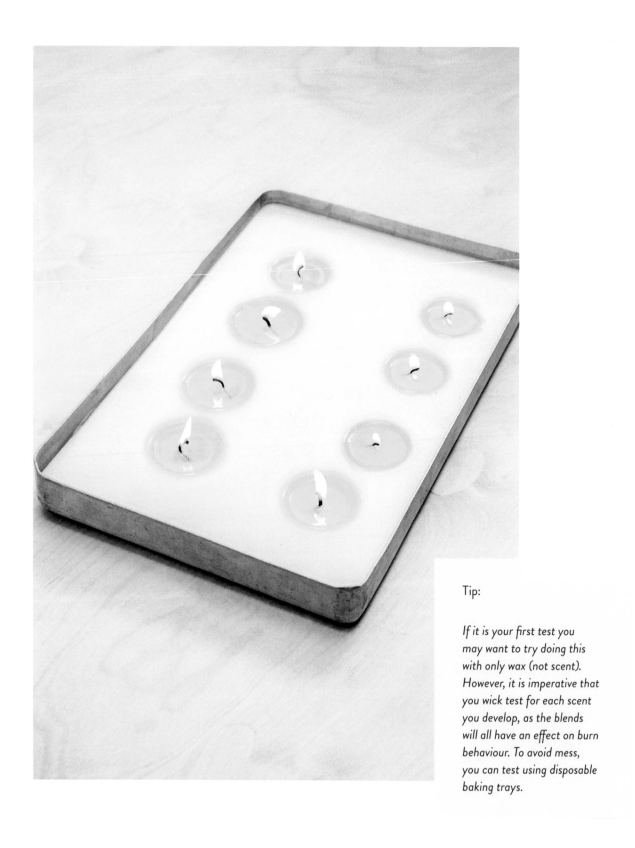

Tip:

If it is your first test you may want to try doing this with only wax (not scent). However, it is imperative that you wick test for each scent you develop, as the blends will all have an effect on burn behaviour. To avoid mess, you can test using disposable baking trays.

Once done and you know which wick to go for, run the exact same test in the containers you're going to be using. Start with wicking your jar (see page 78), pouring the wax into it, letting it set and then check for burn behaviours. By the end of your testing, you should know which wick size works for your candle containers.

WICK BEHAVIOUR TESTING

1. Attach the wicks you want to test at equal 10–12cm (4–4¾ in) intervals in a large baking tray. You can do this with a glue gun, or some wicks come with adhesive clasps. Don't overload a tray as you need to ensure each wick has ample space for the testing. If you are testing a lot of different wicks you may want to separate the different types (wooden, flat, square) into different trays. Ensure you make a diagram of the tray with the size of each wick included. Blend your wax of choice together with your oil blend (if using). Typically you'll use somewhere between a 6 and 12 per cent oil to wax ratio.

2. Once the wicks are set and your wax is ready, pour it into the tray. Think about it as if you're making a large multiple-wicked candle. Wait until the wax has set – we'd recommend at least 48 hours to replicate 'reality'.

3. Trim the wicks to 5mm above the wax height. Once trimmed, light them all at the same time and burn for 2 hours, making sure the tray is in a location free of draughts and on a heat-resistant surface. This timeframe will showcase the basic burning behaviour of each individual wick.

4. Take notes at 15-minute intervals, monitoring flame size and any flickering or clogging. The more notes you make the more informed your final decision will be. If you like, you can even record the whole thing on camera.

5. After two hours, blow out the flames and let it all set. Try not to move the tray around as it will affect how the wax sets. Grab a ruler and measure the diameters of the melt pools, observe the wicks and match it all to the vessels you're going to be using (see pages 46–50).

6. Before you decide which wick is the right one, continue running this test until all the wax in your tray is gone. Keep on making notes and observing burn behaviours.

TYPES OF CONTAINER

There are many different types of vessel that are suitable for pouring a candle into. For our own line, we knew we wanted to use amber jars from the outset because we loved the atmospheric warm glow they provide when the flame is burning, but there are so many options that may be more in keeping with your interior, style or the occasion for which you are creating your candle.

You need to ensure three things when searching for a container for your scented candle. Make sure the vessel is fireproof, seamless and won't leak, and that the material is strong enough to resist high levels of heat and won't crack or break when hot. When it comes to candle safety, any leakage from a crack or a porous material such as terracotta, will result in an exposed wick, which will create a large flame and be a potential fire hazard (see page 136). Naturally, this rules out materials like plastic and wood, but also very delicate types of glass that are likely to shatter if they get too hot.

From here the choice becomes more about the aesthetic you are looking to achieve; this includes the shape of the vessel itself. Generally speaking the best style will have straight sides, meaning the mouth of the vessel is the same diameter as the base. This allows you to find a wick that will create an even melt pool for the candle throughout its life, without risking overheating the jar when the candle burns towards the base.

GLASS

This is most commonly used because it is both heat-resistant and (unless it is coated) it allows you to see the flicker or glow of the flame when burning, which is very atmospheric. With glass it is important to ensure it isn't too delicate and that the base of the vessel is thick enough to withstand heat. Another consideration with glass is that pull-away (where the wax moves away from the side of the container and leaves a gap between the solid wax and jar) is much more visible than within a non-translucent vessel. To minimise this, you will need to take extra care to ensure the vessel is at the right temperature before pouring (see tip).

Tip:

To avoid pull-away, make sure you pour into a vessel at room temperature —around 20°C/68°F; if this is not possible you can warm up the glass vessel with a hairdryer or heat gun.

THE SCENTED CANDLE WORKSHOP

PORCELAIN

This is an extremely tough ceramic material that is fired at a very high temperature to ensure it is non-permeable while still being delicate to the touch. Porcelain works well with glazes, so it can be found in a wide array of colours and finishes. The other great thing about porcelain is that it has some translucency, so when the candle is burning the container gives off a warm glow. Due to its high firing temperatures there is also a low risk of thermal shock (when the container cracks) compared to other types of ceramic vessels.

METAL AND TIN

Metals make an attractive alternative to glass vessels, and can be used to create a sense of luxury, particularly when using a material such as brushed steel or copper. These materials are more durable than glass, so you will not risk cracking, however, you can lose some of the ambience you get from glass because the container has no translucency. It is worth noting that metal can get very hot, so make sure you look after the wick and always place the candle on a heat-resistant surface so as not to damage the furniture.

TERRACOTTA AND CERAMIC

There are also a range of other, porous materials that are worth considering, including terracotta and concrete (see page 50). However, with any of these you do need to bear in mind that melted wax will soak into the pores of the vessel, which can be dangerous, as it can lead to overheating or cracking. If the pot isn't glazed you can easily seal it yourself using a water-based decoupage glue or glaze, painting it all around the inside (there are a number of eco-friendly water-based sealers for concrete or ceramic materials readily available), or make sure you use a low-shrinkage wax when pouring into terracotta as pull-away is common. Most waxes that are listed for container use will be fine.

These pots make beautiful candle holders and can easily be painted to fit with your scent, decoration or interior. If you want to use regular terracotta or ceramic planters there are a few things you need to do before you start pouring. First, a pot that has been created to be used as a planter is very likely to have a hole in the bottom. This hole will need to be plugged – this can be done with silicone, which will ensure that no melted wax can escape. Also be aware that terracotta is generally unglazed, which makes it porous, so you might need to seal it first, as above. Ceramic behaves in a similar way to terracotta, however, ready-made pots are more likely to have been glazed.

Consider the thickness of these vessels and look for straight sides to ensure you can wick them correctly. While hand-thrown vessels are beautiful, they vary in size, so finding a single wick that will work for all of them may be difficult.

CONCRETE

This man-made material has become a big trend in recent years. This simplistic design is often preferred for minimalist interiors, but again, the main thing to consider is that the interior of the vessel is glazed or, if you are making the pot, that you use a water-based concrete seal to finish.

Tip:

Remember, you can always reuse the vessel, either to pour another candle into or as a container or plant pot. Once the candle has burned out, submerge the vessel in a pan of warm water so the remaining wax melts, or put in the oven on a low heat for 5–10 minutes. When the last bits of wax have melted, remove and dispose them, then the vessel can be cleaned and reused. The wick clasp can easily be removed when the jar is warm using a small teaspoon.

SCENT THROW, QUALITY AND CONSISTENCY

The previous sections will have given you a broad understanding of the different oils, waxes, wicks and vessels available to candle makers. We'd recommend you test everything thoroughly over and over again to make sure the scent throws and the burn behaviours of your wax and wicks, and therefore quality of your creation are spot on before gifting. Testing is the fun part and you can enjoy both the process and the results at every stage.

If you are unsure of anything, check in with your chosen suppliers – for wax you should easily be able to find out where it is manufactured and from where the raw materials are sourced, and the same goes for your oils. Any supplier will be able to give you a Material Safety Data Sheet, which will list all of the ingredients and any warnings you should be aware of.

But once you have done all of your due diligence, what do you need to do to ensure your chosen blend throws well and that the wax is both burning correctly and is aesthetically pleasing? There are some simple rules to follow.

First, make sure your blend always adheres to an oil to wax ratio of between 6 and 12 per cent of the total volume of your vessel. Any less than this and you will find it hard to get the candle to throw well or emit any real fragrance into the room; more than this and you will struggle to get the wax to set effectively. The actual percentage will be determined during your testing, and is down to the strength of the materials. If your scent is made up of heavy, woody base notes and strong florals, you are likely to need a lower percentage than if you are looking to create something that is light and delicate made up largely of fresh and citrus notes.

Also consider the type of oils you use. As we have discussed, it is much easier to achieve throw with botanical oils than it is with essential oils only. There is also a cost implication if using essential oils, so the trade-off here will be the throw of the scent in the room.

Then comes the question we get asked most often in our workshops. How do we make the wax smooth?

When you are testing your waxes you will see a lot of different setting behaviours. It is quite common to see what is called frosting, when little spots or crystals appear on the surface of the wax. While frosting doesn't affect burn behaviour or scent throw, it isn't aesthetically pleasing. Unfortunately, this is a common issue with vegetable waxes and it is nothing more than a crystal growth on the edge of the wax. This is less visible when using clear, non-coloured wax but even then there are ways to avoid it. Make sure you don't overheat the wax when melting and that you adhere to the manufacturer guidelines. When blending, stir less vigorously and to reduce the likelihood of frosting, pour from one jug to another a few times before pouring into your vessel. This is to make sure the blend is as perfect as possible and to allow for the candle to throw scent when burning from the very start. You can also reheat the wax surface, which can be done using a hand-held heat gun – these are affordable and a great way to ensure an even finish as they can also remove any cracks.

Another way to ensure overall consistency and a smooth finish on your candles is to top pour. So, rather than fill the candle to the desired height straight away, pour to three-quarters of the desired height and then, once the batch has set, create another jug of your blend to pour on top. This means the wax will set more neatly and ensures a smooth finish.

You may also notice that your candles appear to be sweating. This is very common with soy candles in particular. Again, it won't affect the burn or quality of your candle, but it doesn't look great. Blending vegetable waxes can reduce the effect – using something like beeswax or coconut with soy will help – but another option is to reduce the overall oil percentage. It is also worth ensuring that you pour the candles in a temperature-controlled environment and that they are stored away from excessive heat.

Make sure you don't overheat the wax when melting and that you adhere to the manufacturer guidelines.

EQUIPMENT

Here are the essential parts of your candle-making toolkit. If you're planning on crafting often, we'd suggest buying separate utensils for your candle making.

Measuring jug – to measure the wax and oil.

Your chosen wax – see pages 36–39.

Bain-marie – you can buy this piece of equipment as a double-walled pan, or simply use a heatproof bowl set over a pan of water.

Kitchen thermometer – to double-check the temperature of the wax.

Your oil blend – depending on your profile and choice of oil, you'll need between 6 and 12 per cent.

Digital jeweller's scale – to measure out the oil.

Wicks – you'll want the right size based on the diameters of the containers you're using (see pages 40–43).

Glue gun and sticks – you won't need these if you are using wicks with self-adhesive stickers.

Containers – whichever vessels you want to make your candles with. Clean them before pouring in your wax.

Utensils – a wooden spoon or palette knife to stir the wax with.

Two metal pouring jugs – used to blend the wax and oil.

Pegs – used to centre the wicks once you have completed your pour, we recommend using simple wooden pegs.

Scissors – to cut wicks to size when finishing your candle.

CREATING
A SCENT

If there is one thing we've learnt along the way it is that setting yourself a brief is absolutely essential when you decide to create your own scent. Without it you are simply going to get lost in the vast array of fragrance and essential oils available. The brief will guide you and, more importantly, keep you focused on the story you are trying to convey or the memory you want to recall.

HOW TO CREATE A SCENT

A brief is absolutely essential when you decide to create your own scent.

You can decide to either play in aromatherapy or storytelling. Depending on your decision your brief will look inherently different.

AROMATHERAPY

A brief that plays in aromatherapy will be for the most part straightforward and more solution-driven, which makes most decisions for you before you've even started. Thinking about ingredients and profiles, these will be decided based on what you're creating the scent for. Are you trying to create a candle that will allow you to wind down or are you looking for a scent that will help you get up and be energised? Granted, we've made this sound like it's not as much fun, but it actually is. It is simply more structured by external parameters, that's all.

CALMING SCENTS

Bergamot

Cedarwood

Chamomile

Cinnamon

Frankincense

Geranium

Lavender

Lemon

Rose

Neroli

Petitgrain

Sandalwood

Ylang ylang

Palo Santo

Vetiver

SCENTS THAT AID FOCUS AND CONCENTRATION

Angelica

Clove

Cardamom

Cedarwood

Eucalyptus

Ginger

Peppermint

Sage

ENERGISING SCENTS

Orange

Lime

Grapefruit

Peppermint

Rosemary

Thyme

Basil

Lemongrass

Black pepper

STORYTELLING

Playing in storytelling will enable you to explore more creative routes and allow you to create without conditions, because it is the more abstract, uncontrolled approach. You'll have to think about the story, dive into your limbic system via your nose and try to figure out which scents bring you back to that holiday or moment in life that you want to recreate.

Our core range is based on storytelling, and whenever we work on custom scents for weddings, events and brand partners, we have our go-to standard template that we use as a starting point. The questions that we ask ourselves or our collaborators are:

What's the story you want to tell with this scent?

For our Greenhouse scent, the story was a very personal one; it tells of summers spent in Greece, with grandparents who were known in the village for their tomato plants, which to a teenage kid from a German city was novel.

What pictures, memories and colours do you want to evoke when smelling the oil combination/burning the candle?

Some of the keywords that we wrote down when working on this scent were: summer days, silence, heat, greens and yellows, family time, traditional, familiar, uplifting, happiness . . .

Describe a place, a moment in time or the weather on that given day.

This section is very personal, for Greenhouse we went further into details about a usual day in the Greek village.

Dive further into your thoughts – thinking about background information, you can also look to create a visual mood board, which will really help to bring the scent to life in colour.

Once you have this brief completed and you have created a mood board, there are a number of tools that will help navigate you through the world of fragrance. These tools will help you develop a layered fragrance with depth, but they will also ensure you order and then work with the right oils for your brief.

THE
SCENT
WHEEL
AND
HOW TO
USE IT

We use a blend of botanicals and essential oils in our scents. But regardless of which types of oils you are using there is a tool that will help to categorize the oils into groups, and discover combinations that you might not naturally put together.

This tool is known as the fragrance wheel. There are many versions of the wheel and the first was created by Paul Jellinek in 1949. We have developed our own version of it, but have stuck to the main categories, which are:

– Floral

– Fresh

– Oriental

– Woody

When blending your own scents, refer back to this chapter in conjunction with the scent pyramid on page 66 and the creative brief you've put together for yourself.

To start, it might make sense for you to establish which group you're most drawn to. Think about the scents you like and find out where on the wheel these sit. Usually, we'll end up preferring notes from a couple of categories. This quick exercise helps you somehow ease into using the fragrance wheel. Once you know which categories you like, you can do the same test with the brief you're trying to answer. If you're telling a story, consider which scents trigger those pictures, memories and emotions for you and which groups these sit under. If you find that the notes you've pulled out sit across the entire wheel, focus on a few and aim to build out the areas around it. At the beginning, we'd recommend keeping it simple and straightforward and blending oils that sit in the same or neighbouring groups. You want the first few blends to be successful to keep you blending, rather than frustrate you and make you stop.

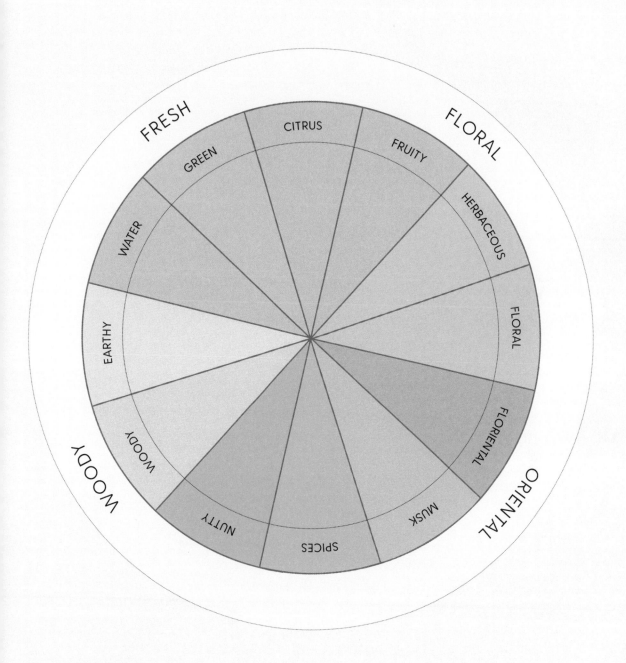

Once you've got a feeling for the oils you're working with, you can be a bit more daring. Try blending things that might seem odd to others but work just fine for you.

Here are some categories and notes that we like that you can use as a starting point:

FRESH

Water: *marine notes, sea salt*
Green: *tomato leaves, cut grass, peppermint, spearmint*
Citrus: *lemongrass, mandarin, tangerine, lemon, orange*
Fruity: *bergamot, blackcurrant, sweet orange, other berries*

FLORAL

Herbaceous: *basil, rosemary, parsley, oregano*
Floral: *rose, lily, geranium, jasmine, ylang ylang, lavender*
Floriental: *orange blossom, tuberose*

ORIENTAL

Musk: *benzoin, clary sage, myrrh, angelica root, labdanum*
Spices: *cinnamon, cloves, anise, cardamom, ginger*
Nutty [sweet]: *pistachio, almond, cocoa, vanilla*

WOODY

Woody: *sandalwood, palo santo, cedarwood, cypress, cade*
Earthy: *oakmoss, vetiver, patchouli, frankincense*

Some fragrance wheels include 'Gourmand' as a stand-alone group, but we've included nutty and fruity notes within our main categories.

Tip:

We've all heard the old adage 'opposites attract', well, much like with flavours and sweet and savoury going well together, the same can be said for scent. Woody notes from the wheel, such as cedarwood, will blend well with a floral note such as jasmine.

THE
SCENT
PYRAMID

_All these layers
will be brought
together into
your final scent._

While you might not necessarily be familiar with the scent pyramid you will probably have heard of top, middle and base notes within a scent, as this language is commonly used within the fragrance and perfumery world.

When it comes to creating a scent, you'll be looking to create three different units, or layers, which are known as the top, middle and base notes. Each layer can include more than one note, and all these layers will be brought together into your final scent.

Top notes

Traditionally, top notes are the first impression of a scent; in perfume, they are what you can smell at the beginning and for anywhere from 5 to about 30 minutes after application. Top notes will traditionally be fresh, bright, sharp and welcoming. They are classified as top notes as they are strong in scent, very volatile and evaporate most quickly. In a candle it is often what you'd pick up on the cold throw. Top notes are the scents that will attract you, but they also operate as smooth transition into the heart of the oil blend. Bergamot, grapefruit, lemon, lime, mandarin, pine and basil are typical top notes.

Middle notes

The middle notes are also referred to as the heart of your blend. Mostly that's because they make up the majority of your scent creation. They appear the moment the top notes evaporate and carry on the story. Middle notes last anywhere between two and four hours. Typically, middle notes are rounder, mellow floral profiles and gentle spices; they could be things like geranium, neroli, rose, nutmeg and cypress.

Base notes

When you hear people referring to a scent as luxurious and deep, that's because the creator has done an excellent job finishing off the scent with base notes. Base notes deepen the scent further and, together with the middle notes, they form the main theme of your scent creation. Once all other notes have evaporated and are gone, these notes remain, giving you the very last impression of the scent. When you apply this logic to candles it is

TOP NOTES

MIDDLE NOTES

BASE NOTES

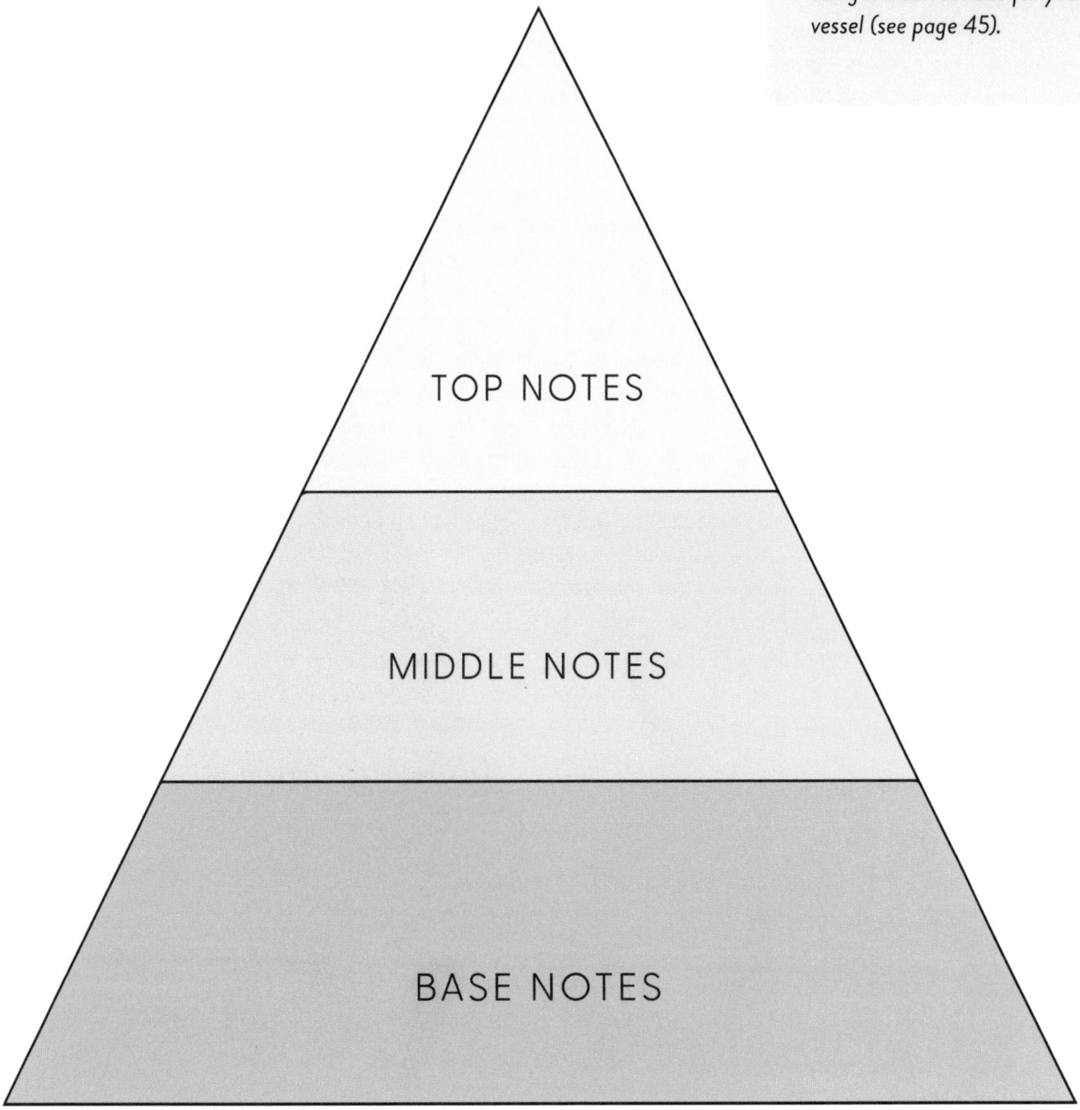

THE SCENTED CANDLE WORKSHOP

often the scent that will linger in the room once you have blown the candle out. Typical base notes are oakmoss, sandalwood, patchouli, benzoin and vanilla.

Layering Scents

When you are creating your own scent for your candle, you'll want to create those entities separate to one another. Once you're happy with your top, middle and base note blends, you take those forward to create your final scent. To check if these work together you can use pH-neutral paper strips. Dip the paper strips into your individual scent elements, using one piece per scent to avoid contamination, and hold them in front of your nose in a layered way, as if you're holding a fan. Hold the paper strip carrying the top notes closer to your nose, followed up by the strip dipped into the middle notes and finally, hold the strip you've dipped into the base notes furthest away from your nose. If you want to keep the base notes really light, you can even hold them in your other hand. Think of this process as using the paper strips to tell yourself and your nose that story of opening, middle and end.

To return again to the example of our Greenhouse scent, we'd worked with a citrusy blend – with lemon zest as the dominant note, which greets you as the cold throw. As you burn through the candle you then experience our light middle notes, with the tomato leaves and basil scent being most dominant here. We kept the base notes to a minimum for this one, so you'll only get a hint of parsley seed coming through. Think of it as a plant, if you wish, taking it from the blossom to the stem and all the way into the root and soil.

Having said all of this, if you prefer to keep it simple and just create a candle that smells of cedarwood, get yourself some cedarwood oil and mix it into your wax.

Creating the blend

When it comes to the composition of the blend that makes up that final oil, there is no hard and fast rule to how your blend should be made. However, as a starting point we suggest making it one third top notes, one third middle notes and one third base notes, and then dialling up or down particular elements depending on the final throw of the scent. It will require patience and a fair amount of trial and error, but that really is the fun part.

Once you have created the blend you desire, you will need to scale the measurements up to make a total of 6–12 per cent of oil to wax ratio. Therefore, if you are working with 1kg (2¼lb) of wax, you should be working with 60–120g (2–4oz) of oil to create the desired throw. The exact percentage will depend on the strength of oils you are working with, for example if your scent is heavy and woody, it is likely you will need a lower percentage of oil when compared with a scent created primarily of lighter citrus notes.

THE
WORKSHOPS

Your candle-making toolkit (see page 54)

Container soy wax – try EcoSoya Advanced or Golden Wax 464 – you'll need 1kg (2¼lb) to make 5 candles.

Your oil blend – depending on your profile and choice of oil, you'll need between 6 and 12 per cent.

Wicks – you'll want the right size based on the diameters of the containers you're using (see pages 40–43).

Containers – for this exercise, they should be the right size to hold a 200g (7oz) candle.

SIMPLE CONTAINER CANDLES

This is it, this is what got us started and it's still the foundation of our line today – soy wax candles in containers. Before you begin, read over the previous chapters dealing with materials, containers and wicks and, of course, scent development.

For the sake of this workshop we will assume the vessels that you're going to make your candles in are all the same size – 200g (7oz) – and all have the same shape. If your chosen vessel varies from this, you will need to scale up or down the percentage accordingly.

If you prefer, you could replace the soy with another vegetable alternative or blend (see pages 36–39).

THE METHOD

1. Start with measuring out the wax you need and place it in the double-walled boiler pan or a heatproof bowl set over a pan of boiling water. Keep a kitchen thermometer in the part of the pan or bowl with the wax at all times, to make sure you're monitoring its temperature throughout the process. Do not overheat.

   While the wax is melting, start preparing the oil blend and the vessels you will be pouring into.

Tip:

When melting the wax you will notice it forms a clump in the middle. Remove the pan from the heat at this point to avoid the wax overheating. If you do overheat it, make sure you allow the wax to cool before adding your oil blend.

2. Start with the vessel. Using your glue gun or stickered wicks, attach the wick to the base of the vessel, making sure it is centred in the jar. You can use a straw to help you hold the wick as you fix it to the base.

3. You can now measure out the scent combination you have created. You will need a digital jeweller's scale for this, to ensure the blend is accurate.

   By this point your wax should have melted. Check to make sure the temperature is between 65 and 75°C (149–167°F). Pour the wax out into one of the metal jugs and set aside to cool a little. Once the temperature of the wax is at a steady 65°C (149°F), you can add your oil blend. Pour it in, stirring slowly clockwise and then anti-clockwise to ensure a thorough blend. We recommend then pouring it into the second metal jug and repeating this process to ensure an evenly distributed blend of oil and wax.

4. Place your wicked jars at even intervals on a tray or on a work surface covered with greaseproof paper – this will reduce any mess from spillage. Push the wick away from the direction of the pour to the side of the vessel – this will stop the wick splitting the flow and reduce any potential spillage.

   You can pour in the wax to the desired height of the vessel (we recommend leaving 5mm (¼ in) from the rim of the vessel, which is the perfect wick height – this is especially important if you are using containers with lids), or you can pour three-quarters of the way up to allow for a top pour once the vessel has set.

Tip:

If you have spilled any wax over the sides of your vessel during the pour, leave it until it has set. It is much easier to clean away once cooled and set.

5. Once you've poured your candles, bring the wick gently back to the centre of the vessel and use the pegs to fix the wick in the centre of your creation. You can buy wick centring devices, which are useful if the diameter of your vessel exceeds the length of a standard peg. Create some friction between the peg and vessel to ensure the wick stays in place as the wax sets. You can do this by pushing the peg against the jar and pulling the wick ever so slightly at the same time.

6. Leave the candles until cool and set, then remove the pegs or wick-centring devices, clean around the vessels if necessary and trim the wicks to size. Now put the candles aside for another 48 hours to cure. The whole thing is pretty much an exercise in patience from start to finish!

You might notice that your candles have little spots or crystals on the surface, this is known as frosting and occurs frequently with soy and other vegetable wax candles. A top pour or reheating (see page 53) will solve this and iron out any cracks that may appear in the top layer of your candle, creating a perfect smooth finish.

Your candle-making toolkit (see page 54)

Container soy wax – try EcoSoya Advanced or Golden Wax 464 – you'll need 1kg (2¼lb) to make 5 candles.

Your oil blend – depending on your profile and choice of oil, you'll need between 6 and 12 per cent.

Wicks – you'll want the right size based on the diameters of the containers you're using (see pages 40–43).

Containers – for this exercise, they should be the right size to hold a 200g (7oz) candle and ideally clear.

Non-toxic PVA glue – to attach the pressed flowers to the inside of your clear container.

Brushes – for spreading the glue onto the inside of the jar.

Gloves – to prevent you getting sticky fingers throughout the process!

A selection of pressed plants – to decorate your vessel with.

BOTANICAL CANDLES

Botanical candles are a lovely way to create a unique aesthetic. By botanical candles, we not only mean a more botanical fragrance profile, but also the decoration of the candle jar with pressed seasonal flora. During this workshop we will give you the expertise to create both elements.

The steps are generally the same as for our simple container exercise on pages 75–79, but you can choose to use any other type of wax base here, too. We recommend using a blend of soy or rapeseed wax with beeswax for this. In other words, you want a wax blend that's soft to give you a long burn time, but steady enough to make sure it doesn't melt all the way to the edges. Sounds a bit unorthodox, but it will all make sense along the way. It's very important to double-check your wick size in accordance to the diameter of your vessels when making a botanical candle – remember, you won't want a clean burn to the edges of this candle because it will damage the botanical decoration.

We recommend using a clear container here so that you can show off the decorative elements of the botanicals. As for the oil blend, you could try something that goes with the botanicals you intend to use. A suggestion of a summery scent, for example, could be our citrusy sweet blend below. When blending this scent, read over the scent wheel and scent pyramid chapters:

Top notes: Sweet orange, mandarin or tangerine, lemon and grapefruit

Middle notes: Peach or apricot and palmarosa

Base notes: Vanilla and sandalwood

Once you're happy with your oil blend, it is time to decorate the jar.

1.   Start with measuring out the wax you need and place it in
      the double-walled boiler pan or a heatproof bowl set over
      a pan of boiling water. Keep a kitchen thermometer in the
      part of the pan or bowl with the wax at all times to make sure
      you're monitoring its temperature throughout the process.
      Do not overheat (see tip on page 75).

      While the wax is melting, start preparing the oil blend and
      the vessels you will be pouring into.

      When decorating the inside of the vessels, as with most
      things in life, less is more. Start with one area of your
      container, distributing the glue with the brush evenly
      on the inside. You only want a thin foundation layer.

2. From then on, dip into your glue, then with the brush select and pick up the blossom or leaf you want to attach first, manoeuvring the brush then placing it onto the first area of your container.

Once in place, apply the glue all over the botanical, making sure it's lying flat against the inside of the vessel. Avoid double layering botanicals and leaves. Repeat with your botanicals until you've got the desired effect. Think about using repetitive patterns or colour coordinate your petals and leaves.

Using your glue gun or stickered wicks, attach the wick to the base of the vessel, making sure it is centred in the jar. You can use a straw to help you fix the wick to the base. Repeat for the other vessels.

You can now measure out the scent combination you have created (see page 58). You will need a digital jeweller's scale for this, to ensure the blend is accurate.

Tip:

Instead of glue, you can also use melted vegetable wax to apply the botanicals to the inside of the vessel. Simply dip your botanicals into your wax using tweezers, then use a brush to press them onto the inside of your container.

3. By this point your wax should have melted. Check to make sure the temperature is between 65 and 75°C (149–167°F). Pour the wax into one of the metal jugs and let cool a little. Once the temperature of the wax is at a steady 65°C (149°F), you can add your oil blend. Pour it in, stirring slowly clockwise and then anti-clockwise to ensure a thorough blend. We recommend then pouring it into the second metal jug and repeating this process to ensure an evenly distributed blend of oil and wax.

    Once the glue has dried and your wax is blended and ready to go, you can begin to pour it into the vessels.

4. Place your wicked jars at even intervals on a tray or on a work surface covered with greaseproof paper. Push the wick away from the direction of the pour to the side of the vessel.

Tip:

If you want to use botanicals from your garden, feel free to do so. Just remember that you want them dried and pressed, not just dried. You can, for instance, harvest lavender at the end of July, press it over the summer and then use it in lavender-scented candles later in the year. Simply place the blossom or leaves in a book and let them dry and become pressed over time.

Make sure you're extra careful when it comes to pouring and take care when it comes to the temperature. You don't want to work with wax that's too hot as it might cause the petals, leaves and blossoms to come off straight away.

5.   You can pour in the wax to the desired height of the vessel (we recommend leaving 5mm from the rim of the vessel, which is the perfect wick height – this is especially important if you are using containers with lids), or you can pour three-quarters of the way up to allow for a top pour once the vessel has set (see page 53). Remember, for this particular candle you don't want a clean burn as you need a safety rim of wax going all around the jar, to ensure your decorations remain intact.

Once you've poured your candles, bring the wick gently back to the centre and use the pegs to fix the wick in the centre of your vessel. Create some friction between the peg and vessel to ensure the wick stays in place as the wax sets. You can do this by pushing the peg against the jar and pulling the wick ever so slightly at the same time.

If a botanical comes away and floats in your melt-pool while burning your candle, blow out the flame and pick out the item, as it can become highly hazardous if left to catch.

Measuring scales – to measure the wax.

Beeswax – you'll want just 1.5kg (2¼lb) of beeswax as we're not going to use fragrance here; beeswax will give you the long burn time and a slight natural scent.

Two tall metal or aluminium containers – whatever you use, be willing to sacrifice the containers to your candle-making plans! Our containers were 30cm (12 in) high and 16cm (6¼ in) in diameter.

A stainless steel pot – to place your wax container in, like a bain marie.

Kitchen thermometer – to check the temperature of the wax.

Wicks – you need either square or flat long cotton wicks on a spool that you can cut to size yourself.

Scissors – for cutting wicks to size and trimming them when finishing off the candles.

Metal nuts – to attach to the end of your wicks as weights to keep them straight when dipping. Alternatively, you can use mid-sized stones tied to the end of the wick.

Wooden stick or dowel – to suspend the wick and candles as you dip them.

Old newspapers or cloths – to protect your work surface.

Bucket of cold water – to cool the wax between dips.

A rack or old clothes rail – to hang dipped candles from while setting.

TAPER CANDLES

Hand-dipped tapers are mostly made out of beeswax, so the following instructions are based on that type of wax. While reading the method, you'll realise why a softer vegetable wax isn't really the best option here.

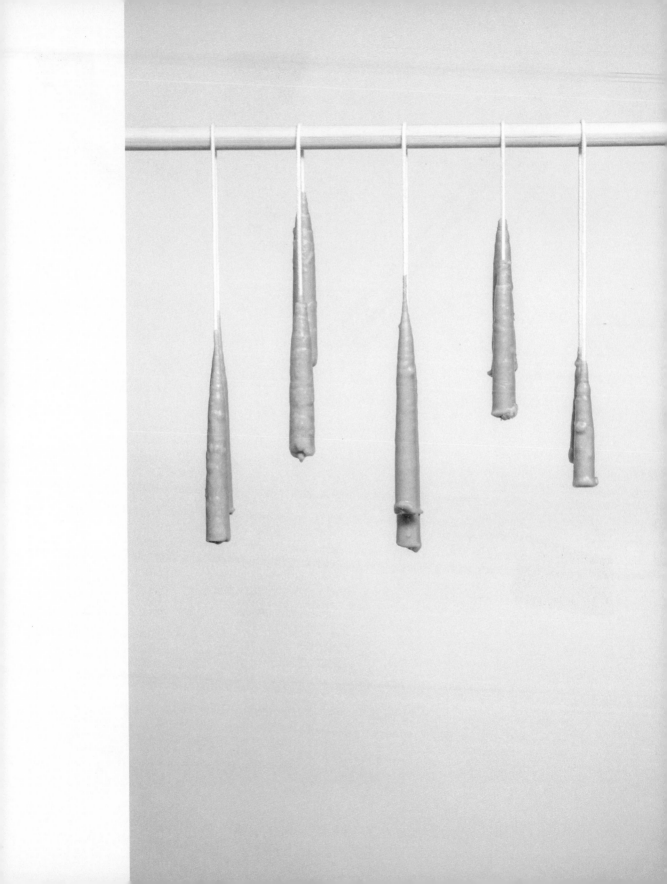

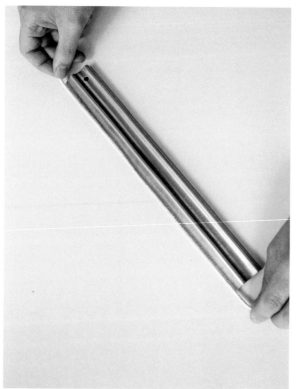

THE SCENTED CANDLE WORKSHOP

1.   Measure out the wax and start melting it using one of the tall containers and the pot. You want to keep your wax heated to make sure it doesn't solidify throughout the process – try to maintain a temperature of around 75°C (167°F) degrees at all times. Fill the other tall container with cold water.

     Before you cut your wicks to size, make sure you don't exceed the depth of the container you're working with. Let's assume you're making 25cm (10 in)-long candles; since we'll be making two tapers at any one time, you want to cut a bit over double the length of one taper and fold it, for dipping into the wax bucket. In other words, cut a piece of wick to a length of 58–62cm (23–24½ in).

2.   To keep the wick straight while dipping, you'll use a metal nut or stone weight tied to both cut ends. These are only needed at the beginning and once your wicks and candles are heavy enough to remain straight while dipping into the wax, you can cut them off.

Tip:

Use a large bucket filled with cold water to speed up the cooling process. Dipping the candles into this in between wax dips will let the wax solidify quicker.

3. Now the wax is melted, the wicks have been cut to size, folded and the weights have been attached to them, you're good to go. It can get messy now, so lay out old newspapers over your work surface.

With the folded wick centred on a stick or dowel, dip the wicks into the melted wax, wait a moment or two, then lift them out, let the excess drip away, and dip them into the water to help the wax to set. Continue dipping and setting until you get to the desired candle thickness.

Cut the weights off the ends of the candles, then dip them a few times into the wax to seal them. Don't cut the joined wicks yet – use this piece to hang the candles on the rack to harden.

Tip:

If you want all of your
taper candles to be the
same length, you'll need
to top up your bucket with
more melted beeswax as
you work, as the levels will
slowly go down.

4. Keep your tapers hanging up in pairs and wrap them up together until you want to use
    them, then cut through the wick before use. If you find that they've developed bloom
    (when the wax looks almost powdery rather than a shiny yellow), don't worry about it,
    this happens occasionally when using 100 per cent beeswax, but won't affect the quality
    of your taper.

WELLNESS CANDLES

During this workshop we are going to focus purely on the aromatherapy element, helping you to create a candle using only essential oils. The idea here is to make a candle that will make you feel a certain way, whether that is relaxed and calm in preparation for rest, or invigorated and energised as part of a morning yoga session. This candle is made out of coconut and soy wax blend and 100 per cent essential oils.

Let's make a candle that will lift the mood. We'll keep this simple; everything you need is all listed in the simple container candle exercise (see page 74), but since we're working on a scent that's going to be uplifting, here's a recommended essential oil blend for you to work with:

7g (1¹/₃ teaspoon) lavender

5g (1 teaspoon) bergamot

2g (¹/₃ teaspoon) grapefruit

1g lemon (¹/₆ teaspoon)

1g spearmint (¹/₆ teaspoon)

2g (¹/₃ teaspoon) clary sage

The quantities above are enough to make one 200g (7oz) candle (or two 100g/3½ oz candles). You can adjust some of the citrusy notes as long as the overall quantities stay the same; if you don't like lavender try neroli, jasmine or ylang ylang instead.

To create the candle, follow the steps on page 77–81, using 200g (7oz) wax (100g/3½ oz each of soy wax and coconut wax). Remember that the throw of this candle won't necessarily fill a room, you are creating this for its aromatherapeutic benefits.

Tip:

You could also try using this same essential oil blend in an ultrasonic diffuser or with an oil burner.

WEDDING CANDLES

Whether it's the venue, the food, the entertainment or the wedding favours, what the bride and groom are searching for more and more is personalisation to make their big day even more memorable. Scent is just another way to do this, and that can go way beyond the perfume the bride wears on the day. Creating a scent for a wedding day is a great way to give the happy couple something very personal, and as scent and memory are so closely linked, will ensure that day lives on.

We have worked with a number of couples to create custom scents for their day. The fragrance you make can be used throughout the venue, as a table centrepiece and, of course, as wedding favours.

SCENT DEVELOPMENT

Start by creating your own scent. To do so, you'll want to set yourself a brief as a couple. As outlined in Chapter 3, Creating a Scent, think about what story you want to tell, and the memories you want to evoke and return to. The inspiration could be your first date, the place where you got engaged, or it could spark memories of your first holiday together. Alternatively, you can take inspiration from the wedding venue.

You can work on the brief as a couple or give the task to your friends during hen dos, celebrations and pre-wedding festivities to see who comes up with the most moving scent.

If you're getting married during spring/summer and want to create something that will go beautifully with the location, and that will remind your guests of the occasion months after the wedding, you can use green scents such as cut grass, juniper, basil, mint or even apple notes. If you want to tell a more romantic story, think about blossoms and florals such as rose, lily of the valley, jasmine and geranium.

For ocean-like scents, trial a combination of peppermint, eucalyptus, pear, lily, mint and lime.

For scents that will evoke memories of warm summer days, think about citrusy notes such as lemon and orange blossom, floral notes like sunflower and ylang-ylang, or dry scents like cedarwood and jasmine.

Tip:

With scent and memory being closely linked, why not create smaller versions of your wedding scent for your guests to take away with them. This is another thing you can create together, as a couple, then you can either bottle up the scent into little vials or diffusers (see page 117), or use it to make little travel candles (see page 110).

CENTREPIECE

Using the standard method (see page 72), you can make a candle in a special container that means something to you, or that you can keep and reuse for years after the wedding celebrations. It could be a unique vintage find or something that has been in the family for decades. By refilling it with the scent of your wedding over and over again, it will be a constant reminder of your special day. Just remember to follow the guidelines listed on page 46–50 when choosing your pot. If the vessel happens to be clear, why not decorate it with petals and botanicals that have been used in the wedding bouquet or in arrangements, and then pressed and dried (see page 88)?

For a large vessel you can use multiple wicks. Just remember to carry out a wick behaviour test (page 45) to ensure you use the best quantity and placement of wicks. You can buy wick centring devices, which are useful if the diameter of your vessel exceeds the length of a standard peg, or you can improvise, as we have here.

Alternatively, you can use homemade taper candles as centrepieces. Again, you could make the tapers with your friends or just as a couple prior to the wedding.

Your candle-making toolkit – see page 54

Container vegetable wax – such as soy, rapeseed or coconut. You'll need just over 500g (1lb) to make 5 candles.

Your oil blend – depending on your profile and choice of oil, you'll need between 6 and 12 per cent.

Wicks – you'll want the right size based on the diameters of the containers you're using (see pages 40–43).

Containers – small tins or jars – they need to be the right size to hold a 100g (3½oz) candle.

TRAVEL CANDLES

Travel is our personal inspiration, with each of the scents that we create based on a place that inspires us, but we have also learnt that many people want to feel at home wherever they are, and what better way to do it than by creating a travel candle to take away with you? During this workshop we will help you to create a scent that gives you a sense of home regardless of where you rest your head.

For most of us, home is somewhere where we relax, recharge and feel at ease. With that in mind the scent that we're going to create here will reflect the feelings of being safe and cosy while being away.

You can, of course, flip this approach on its head and create a scent to remind you of a meaningful holiday. Think about the earlier chapter on Fragrance and Memory, especially around the brief you'll set yourself, and see what scents evoke the right emotions and memories for you.

This candle will be made out of vegetable wax and 100 per cent essential oils. It's the same method as for simple container candles (page 72), the only difference is adjusting the quantities to create a smaller version that you can pop into your hand luggage and take away on your explorations.

Here's a recommended essential oil blend for you:

5g (1 teaspoon) lavender

3g (¹/₂ teaspoon) chamomile

2g (¹/₃ teaspoon) rosemary

If you want to switch it up, replace the chamomile with marjoram, or add ginger or sandalwood for stress relief to give the scent more depth. If you need the ultimate relaxation add valerian and… goodnight. But don't leave your candle unattended while you sleep!

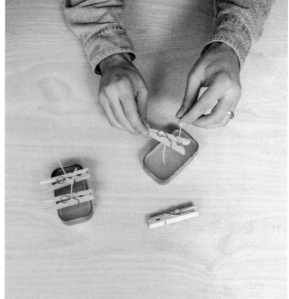

THE METHOD

1. Start with measuring out the wax you need and place it in the double-walled boiler pan or a heatproof bowl set over a pan of boiling water. Keep a kitchen thermometer in the part of the pan or bowl with the wax at all times to make sure you're monitoring its temperature throughout the process. Do not overheat.

2. While the wax is melting, you can prepare the vessels you will be pouring into. Using your glue gun or stickered wicks, attach the wick to the base of the vessel, making sure it is centred in the vessel. You can use a straw to help you fix the wick to the base.

    You can now measure out the scent combination you have created. You will need a digital jeweller's scale for this, to ensure the blend is accurate.

3. By this point your wax should have melted. Check to make sure the temperature is between 65 and 75°C (149–167°F). Pour the wax out into one of the metal jugs and set aside to cool a little. Once the temperature of the wax is at a steady 65°C (149°F), you can add your oil blend. Pour it in, stirring slowly clockwise and then anti-clockwise to ensure a thorough blend. We recommend then pouring it into the second metal jug and repeating this process to ensure an evenly distributed blend of oil and wax.

    Place your wicked vessels at even intervals on a tray or on a work surface covered with greaseproof paper in case of spillage. Push the wick away from the direction of the pour to the side of the vessel – this will stop the wick splitting the flow and reduce any potential spillage.

    You can pour in the wax to the desired height of the vessel (we recommend leaving 5mm from the rim of the vessel, which is the perfect wick height – this is especially important if you are using containers with lids), or you can pour three-quarters of the way up to allow for a top pour once the candle has set.

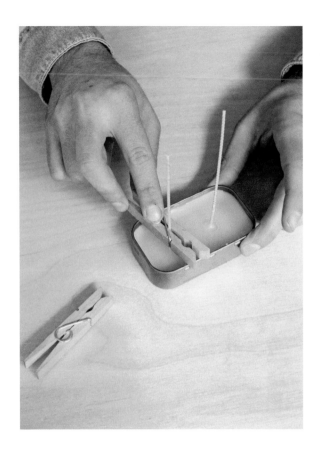

4. Once you've poured your candles, bring the wick gently back to the centre of the vessel and use the pegs to fix the wick in the centre of your creation. Create some friction between the peg and vessel to ensure the wick stays in place as the wax sets.

5. Leave the candles until cool and set, then remove the pegs, clean around the vessels if necessary and trim the wicks to size. Now put the candles aside for another 48 hours to cure.

Tip:

Turn your relaxing holiday candle scent into a mist using distilled water and your essential oil blend, pour into a little atomiser and spritz away while travelling to stay calm and relaxed.

FESTIVE CANDLES

Candles are for life, not just for Christmas. But it goes without saying that they make wonderful gifts and over the longer nights there is nothing better than cosying up on the sofa with a scented candle to really get you into the festive spirit.

We'll assume that you want the maximum Christmas effect, which is why we'll pair this make with the botanical candle workshop (see page 80). Nonetheless, if you're more of a minimalist and not big into decorations, the next few steps work perfectly fine with our Simple Container Candle, too (see page 72).

This candle will be made out of vegetable wax, and because we want this scent to fill the room, we'll need to work with a blend of botanical and essential oils.

A suggestion of Christmas scent could be this traditional blend below. When blending this scent, refer to the scent wheel on page 62 and the scent pyramid on page 66:

Top notes: Orange and pine

Middle notes: Ginger, cinnamon and clove

Base notes: Fir and sandalwood

For a Christmas decoration, you could use pressed rosemary, fennel or ferns. You could also use poinsettia for the ultimate festive feel. You can use the dried plants to decorate a large clear vessel, just remember the wick ratio discussed on page 83 – you don't want the candle to burn all the way to the edge of the vessel if you're decorating it.

Tip:

You could split this into different scents and burn them separately for a more stripped-down version, or together to create the ultimate festive mood. This will also allow you to create gifts for the whole family but without everyone getting the same scent.

SEASONAL SCENTS

Fragrance can take you back to a particular place and time, and it is also a great trigger for the senses to remind you of a particular season. As with a Christmas candle, specific scents such as clove or cinnamon make us feel festive and wintry, and the same idea can be applied to every season throughout the year.

So in this workshop we will provide you with inspiration to create a candle for each season. We don't necessarily suggest burning them within that season exclusively, because you might prefer to be reminded of warm summer evenings in the middle of winter – but that's just a thought.

Follow the steps listed in the Simple Container Candle Workshop (see page 72). You may want to use a different type of vegetable wax, such as rapeseed, beeswax, coconut or a blend. Remember that some of these waxes already have a scent, which might play into your scent profile. If they don't work with the fragrance you want to create, perhaps stick to soy or rapeseed, which are odourless.

On the following pages you'll find some starter thoughts for seasonal scent development.

SPRING

Think about the feelings that spring evokes for you. It could be a new beginning, the smell of freshness and where that takes you personally, or green scents to nod to the awakening of nature. Once you have this basis you can refer to the scent wheel on page 65 to come up with interesting combinations.

Citrus, Fresh and Floral categories should be your go-to here – think of cut grass, delicate floral blossom or fragrances that evoke memories of cleanliness, such as aquatic notes.

SUMMER

We can't help but think about sun, sand and the ocean, juicy fruits, sweet ice creams and the heat, but where does summer take you? During summer months, candles aren't as popular, at least not in the UK, but they are a great accompaniment to the perfect al fresco meal. Think of using strong scents with a focus on nature-mimicking oils to ensure maximum throw. Go large with the vessel, testing multiple wick candles so it fills the air with scent.

Try Fruity notes like berry, mimosa or orange blossom, heady Florals such as tuberose, and Orientals including sandalwood and oud.

Tip:

You could also add citronella to keep the bugs away, meaning your al fresco meal can last well into the evening.

AUTUMN

This season makes us think of golden-orange colours, crisp and cold days and warm spicy scents. Think about foodie notes here – warm apple, pumpkin spices, coffee and vanilla. If you want to steer clear of things that seem too sweet, why not go for hops, hemp and a hint of amber.

WINTER

While we have already given you hints and tips to create a Christmas candle on page 118, there is so much more to winter. It's all about being indoors and cosy.

For a less traditional festive but ultimate indoors scent, try a blend of labdanum, vetiver, rosemary, woodsmoke, cade and benzoin.

Tip:

You may want to try a different vessel here. Metal and tin really come into their own at this time of year, with brass and copper vessels adding a sense of luxury to your interior.

CANDLE SAFETY

Candle safety is something that is often overlooked, but it's very important. Throughout the development of your candles we highly recommend the testing of all elements used within the process, including the wax, the wicks and, of course, the vessel.

However, even when you have done all of these things it is important to look after the candle throughout its life. Here are some simple things to monitor and look out for whenever you burn a candle.

Before each burn it is essential to ensure you have removed any unnecessary burnt wick, trimming the wick to approximately 5mm above the wax top. This is really easy and can be done simply by pinching away the burnt wick with your fingers, before it is lit. This will also ensure the candle doesn't give off any nasty black smoke and will avoid the wick turning in on itself and causing what is known as mushrooming. Mushrooming creates a larger flame, which at best will burn through your candle much faster than it should but at worst can overheat the container.

When lighting a candle, make sure that no wick trimmings or used matches are in the wax, always burn your candle on an even and fire-resistant surface and ensure that it is away from flammable items such as plants, magazines, books and fabrics. If you are unsure if the surface is fireproof it is worth putting a coaster underneath the jar.

When burning your scented candle for the first time, allow the wax to melt all the way to the edge of the vessel. This will usually take between 30 minutes to an hour. Doing so will ensure an even burn throughout the candle and will avoid what is known as tunnelling, where only the central part of the wax melts, creating a shorter burn time.

Never burn the candle for longer than four hours at a time, regardless of the wax type used. Burning for longer than this can overheat the vessel, and the wax will burn through much faster than it should. When you extinguish the candle always ensure you leave it on an even surface as the container may be hot. Never extinguish a candle with

Tip:

Place your candle inside a large hurricane jar for increased safety – it helps to avoid flickering from airflow within the room, particularly where there is a lot of movement around it. To create a decorative hurricane jar, find a wide-based, clear glass jar or vase, fill the base with 5–7.5cm (2–3 in) of non-flammable decorative sand and place the candle inside.

water, it can cause hot wax to splatter and might cause the glass container to break. Extinguish the candle if it repeatedly smokes, flickers or if the flame becomes too high. If this occurs the candle isn't burning properly. Let it cool, trim the wick and then check for draughts before relighting.

When the candle is down to 1cm (⅓ in), discontinue use, because at this point the wick will be close to the end of its life, reaching the metal clasp and the naked flame will be very close to the surface of the vessel, which can cause overheating.

Remember to always burn your candle within sight, away from draughts, and never leave it unattended. Please keep it out of reach of children and pets.

RESOURCES

STOCKISTS AND SUPPLIERS

Everyone has a different take on scent, so it's important to do your own research and find the right manufacturer for the blends you want to create. But here are some suggestions for places to get started with sourcing oils, wax and equipment.

4 CANDLES UK

Fragrance oils, wax and wicks.
www.4candles.co.uk

SCENTYMENTAL

Fragrance oils.
www.scentymental.co.uk

PERFUMER'S WORLD

*Essential oils and
fragrance oils.*
www.perfumersworld.co.uk

MUJI

Essential oils.
www.muji.eu

NEAL'S YARD

Essential oils.
wwww.nealsyardremedies.co.uk

Tip:

*For candle making
equipment and tools,
don't overlook Amazon
and eBay.*

GLOSSARY

Base notes – The heaviest part of the scent that in combination with the middle note creates the main theme of a scent. Base notes add depth to a fragrance and are usually heavy and deep – think woody and musk scents.

Botanical candles – Candles that are adorned with botanical elements, such as leaves and petals as a means of decoration.

Clogging – This occurs when the wick isn't strong enough for the vessel and it will not light again between burns because it has been engulfed by wax.

Cold throw – The smell of the candle from the vessel before it is lit.

Essential oil – Oil extracted from flowers, roots, twigs, peels, seeds and barks of plants and trees or grasses, to name a few.

Flash point – The temperature at which a fragrance oil becomes combustible if exposed to a flame or spark. Generally when blending with waxes, fragrances with a low flash point are still safe to use, but it is recommended to use waxes with a high melting point.

Fragrance oil – An oil made from blended synthetic aroma compounds or natural essential oils, that are diluted with a carrier oil such as vegetable or mineral oils or propylene glycol.

Frosting – A naturally occuring crystallisation of vegetable wax as it sets and attempts to return to its natural state. Creates a frost-like appearance on the top or sides of your candle. Also known as polymorphism.

Hot throw – The scent emitted from a candle when it is lit.

Melting point – The point at which the solid wax flakes become liquid, ready for blending with your scent blend. It is also the point at which your finished candle will melt and emit scent.

Melt pool – Refers to the area of melted wax within your candle. Ideally with container candles you are looking to achieve a full melt pool, whereby the wax melts to the edge of the vessel, resulting in a clean burn.

Middle notes – The heart of the fragrance, these notes work to round or soften the base notes and will appear after the initial top notes fade. Floral notes such as rose or tuberose will often be middle notes.

Mushrooming – Refers to the shape of the wick after the candle has been blown out, where the wick is too large for the vessel. It occurs when the wick picks up more wax than it can burn, which then builds up as a carbon top on the wick. If you see this within your burn testing at the vessel stage, you should retest and find a more suitable wick.

Oil to wax ratio – The percentage of your oil blend to the total volume of wax. This should typically be between 6 and 12 per cent.

Pull away – Shrinkage of wax from the side of the vessel, these air pockets do not affect the quality or the throw of the candle in any way and will disappear when the candle is being used.

Scent throw – The name given to the fragrance emitted from a candle.

Top notes – These are what could be described as the first impression; they are often what is smelt first out of the vessel, when the candle is cold. They are the lightest notes, in a scent combination and will fade first – typically citrus notes and described as light or fresh.

REFERENCES

[1] https://core.ac.uk/download/pdf/13235969.pdf

[2] https://archive.org/stream/in.ernet.dli.2015.502932/2015.502932.A-History_djvu.txt

[2.1] http://ezinearticles.com/?The-History-of-Scented-Candles&id=6352559

[3] https://iakal.wordpress.com/2016/01/02/alexander-the-great-and-the-silk-roads/

[4] Stewart, Susan. *Cosmetics & Perfumes in the Roman World*. Tempus, 2007, pp. 9–13.

[5] https://pdxscholar.library.pdx.edu/cgi/viewcontent.
cgi?referer=&httpsredir=1&article=2015&context=open_access_etds

[6] al-Hassan, Ahmad Y., *Science and Technology in Islam: Technology and applied sciences*.
UNESCO, 2001. pp. 65–69.

[7] al-Hassan, Ahmad Y. "Alcohol and the Distillation of Wine in Arabic Sources". History of
Science and Technology in Islam. Archived from the original on 29 December 2015. Retrieved 19
April 2014.

[8] http://www.gallowglass.org/jadwiga/herbs/hungarywater.html

[8.1] https://perfumesociety.org/history/perfume-crusaders-and-the-renaissance/

[9] https://www.millhousecandles.com/history.php

[10] https://perfumesociety.org/history/louis-xiv-the-sweetest-smelling-king-of-all/

[11] Golan, Tal. *Laws of Men and Laws of Nature: The History of Scientific Expert Testimony in
England and America*. Harvard University Press, 2004. pp. 89–91.

[12] https://guerlainperfumes.blogspot.com/p/history.html

[12.1] https://www.pbs.org/wgbh/nova/article/dogs-sense-of-smell/

[13] https://sciencing.com/human-nose-works-5477127.html

[14] https://www.sciencedirect.com/topics/neuroscience/olfactory-receptor

[15] https://www.pbs.org/wgbh/nova/article/dogs-sense-of-smell/

[16] Arshamian A, Iannilli E, Gerber JC, Willander J, Persson J, Seo H-S, Hummel T, & Larsson M. "The functional neuroanatomy of odor evoked autobiographical memories cued by odors and words." *Neuropsychologia 51* (2013), pp. 123–131.

Herz RS, Eliassen J, Beland S, & Souza T. "Neuroimaging evidence for the emotional potency of odor-evoked memory." *Neuropsychologia 42* (2004), pp. 371–378.

[17] "Fragrances are Not Just Pleasant Odor", Environmental Health Coalition of Western Massachusetts leaflet.

[18]https://www.chagrinvalleysoapandsalve.com/blog/posts/why-are-synthetic-fragrance-oils-so-popular/

https://www.naturesgardencandles.com/blog/what-are-fragrance-oils-made-of/

[19] Burr, Chandler. "Synthetic No.5" *The New York Times*. August 27, 2006. (August 30, 2012), Environmental Working Group. "Not So Sexy: Hidden Chemicals in Perfume and Cologne." May 2010. (August 30, 2012) http://www.ewg.org/notsosexy, Turin, Luca and Sanchez, Tania. *Perfumes: The Guide.* Viking Publishing, 2008.

[20] http://enacademic.com/dic.nsf/enwiki/14644

[21] Rezaei, Karamatollah, Tong Wang, Lawrence A. Johnson. "Hydrogenated vegetable oils as candle wax". *Journal of the American Oil Chemists' Society*. Volume 79, Issue 12, December 2002, pp. 1241–1247

[22] http://candles.org/elements-of-a-candle/wicks/

[23] http://www.fragrancesoftheworld.com/Home

ACKNOWLEDGEMENTS

Where to start? This journey has been all-encompassing for us. We had no idea when we took our first market stall where it would lead. Since 2014 we have made many new friends, learnt something new every day, and fallen completely in love with the world of scent, candle creation and, more broadly speaking, the business.

A huge thank you to all of the customers who have visited our market stall and stores, shopped online or attended one of our candle-making workshops over the last half a decade. The kind words you have given us, and the support you have shown has always been so encouraging. To Adam Reed, we often wonder where we would be had you not passed by Netil Market that first day. You gave us the confidence to keep going and have become a true friend and mentor. To all of our stockists, brand partners and our community – thanks for the support, we know you share our story and that means the world to us.

To our families, you taught us that hard work and dedication pay off in the end, we have you to thank for our work ethic and grounding and we love you all dearly. To our friends, we know we don't see you as much, and visiting us in our studio isn't always that fun, but thanks for doing it anyway. We know you always have our backs and are constantly looking for ways to help us realise our dream. To our LA crew, seeing your limitless ambition and amazing talent has inspired us to keep pushing ourselves.

Shout out to the wonderful #TeamEarl both past and present, thanks for being on this journey, for being open, honest and quite simply rad! Shout out to Megan for being there from the start, for holding it down so we could have the occasional 'day off' and for helping us realise this dream. To Oscar, the best Frenchie in the world, we know you are the one really running the studio and store and that many of our regulars have come just to hang out with you.

To all the other independent businesses, dreamers and doers we have met along the way. Watching many of the people we started with grow and develop has been so cool and inspiring. We feel so privileged to have got to know you. Netil Market – much more than a place, it's a community. We love all of the people we started with there and it will forever be our special place.

To everyone at Kyle Books and Octopus, but especially Tara O'Sullivan and Isabel Gonzalez-Prendergast for making this happen. You have given us a platform to share our passion with others and believed in us since discovering us at one of our classes. Writing this book has been a dream come true and working with you has been an absolute pleasure. To Anna & Tam, thank you for taking our vision and turning it into a reality, we love your work and you've captured our business perfectly. To Abi, thanks for all your design work on this book, we are over the moon with the end result.

A special thank you to Sarah Bates, you were the one to accept our first stall application, you encouraged us to turn a container into a shop. You have long been one of our best candle customers and are always on hand for photo shoots and general advice. But more than all of that, you have become a dear friend.